Trumpet Tunes and Marches

Majestic Organ Processionals for Weddings
Compiled and Edited by Lyndell Leatherman

Table of Contents

TRUMPET TUNE

Swell: Solo Trumpet 8'
Great: 8', 4', 2', Mixture
Choir: 8', 4', 2', Sw. to Gt.
Pedal: 16', 8', Gt. to Ped.

Frederick Swann

Solo
8vb
poco rit.
Gt. (as before)
a tempo
3

(Add mixtures and reeds)
Gt.
Sw.
Solo
poco rit.
8vb
Gt.
a tempo
3

Great/Choir: Contrasting Cornets V
Swell: Flutes 8′, 2′
Pedal: Heavy 16′, 8′

(8′, 2′ or 8′, 4′, 1-1/3′)
(simile)
Gt.
Ch.
(simile)
Gt.
Ch.
Gt.
rit.
Ch.
Original Registration
a tempo
Solo
Gt.
Ped.

Solo
8vb
poco rit.
a tempo
3
(Add mixtures and reeds)
Gt.

a tempo
Sw.
Solo
poco rit.
Gt.
ff
8vb
ff
3
Solo
rit.
Gt.

To Gifford Coombs

WEDDING MARCH

(Recessional)

Richard Purvis (ASCAP)
Edited by Jonas Nordwall

Swell: Principals 8', 4', 2', Mixtures, Sw. to Gt.
Great: Principals 8', 4', 2', Mixtures
Choir: 8' Solo, full-bodied Reed
Pedal: Foundations 16', 8', 4'

Performance note: if played on a four-manual instrument, use Solo: 8' loud Reed coupled to Choir. Use Choir principals coupled to Great and Choir unison off to allow only the solo Reed playable on the Choir manual.

Maestoso ♩ = 106

Add Swell
Reeds
13
Gt.
Ch.
Gt.
Close Swell Box
17
Ch.
simile
Gradually Open Swell Box
22
26
Gt.
Ch.
md 1
Ch.
Gt.

31
Gt.
marcato
Fine
Ch.
Gt.
marcato
marcato
All manuals: Foundations 8', 4', 2'
Couplers: Sw. and Ch. to Gt.
36
Gt.
mf
Sw. Add Reeds 8', 4'
(Box 1/2 open)
40
f
44
Sw. Add Mixtures
D.S. al Fine
cresc. poco a poco

TRUMPET TUNE

Swell: Full
Great: Full with Trumpet
Pedal: 16', Sw. to Ped. 8'

Gordon Young

simile
no rit.
Gt.
ff

TRUMPET AIR

Swell: Solo Trumpet 8'
Great: Principals 8', 4', 2', Mixture IV
Choir: Diapasons 8', 4'
Pedal: Full 16', 8

Henry Purcell
Arranged by Fred Bock

Majestically

13
1
tr
17
2
tr
Gt.
ff
7
21
25
tr
tr
slowing
sfz
fff

For the wedding of Donna Day and Dan Lovestrand

TRUMPET PROCESSIONAL

Swell: Solo Trumpet 8'
Great: Principals 8', 4', 2', Mixture IV
Choir: Diapasons 8', 4'
Pedal: Full 16', 8

Roy Brunner

In a stately manner

11
Sw.
14
2nd time: rit.
Fine
17
Sw.
mp
21
D.C. al Fine

ALLEGRO DI TROMBA

Swell: Trumpet 8'
Great: Diapasons 8', 4'
Pedal: Full 16', 8'; Gt. to Ped. 8'

Benedetto Marcello
Arr. by Rick Parks

Allegro ♩ = ca. 80

7
Sw.
(Gt.)
10
Gt.
13
Sw.
(Gt.)
3
15
3

18
Sw.
Gt.
Gt.
21
Sw.
(Gt.)
23
3
25
Gt.
Sw.

28
31
Gt.
33
Sw.
36
Gt.
rit.
tr

For Sue Ellen and David

TRUMPET TUNE IN F

Swell: Solo Trumpet 8'
Great: Principals 8', 4'
Choir: Diapasons 8', 4'
Pedal: Full 16', 8'

Roy Brunner

13
tr
Gt. Reed Chorus, Mixtures
17
Gt.
Ch. p
Gt. f
manuals only
22
Ch. p
Gt. f
Ch. p
27
Gt. f
tr
32
Sw. f detached

Opening registration
37
Sw.
f
Gt.
41
45
Gt.
mp
Sw.
f
Gt.
Full Organ
Gt.
49
rit.

For Doug, Julia, Jason and Jordan Ellenberg

FESTIVE TRUMPET TUNE

Carolyn Hamlin (ASCAP)

Swell: Viola 8', Bourdon 8', Principal 4', Mix. IV
Great: Diapason 8', Harmonic Flute 8', Octave 4', Fifteenth 2', Mix. IV, Sw. to Gt. 8'
Choir: Festival Trumpet 8'
Pedal: Bourdon 16', Violone 16', Waldhorn 16', Gt. to Ped. 8', Sw. to Ped. 8'

Brisk and stately ♩ = 120

15
Ch.
Gt.
20
tr
25
Gt.
Ch.
Gt.
30

35
40
Gt.
45
Ch.
Gt.
50
Gt.

Sw. Add Reeds 16', 8', 4'
Gt. Add Tromba 8'
Ped. Add Diapason 16', Reed 16', Mix. IV

75
Gt.
Gt.
80
Ch.
Gt.
Gt.
85
Ch.
Gt.
slight rit.
90
Full Organ
Gt.
fff
slowing to end

IMPERIAL MARCH IN C

Op. 32

Swell: Solo Trumpet 8'
Great: Full 8', 4', 2'
Choir: Diapasons 8', 4'
Pedal: Full 16', 8'; Gt. to Ped. 8'

Edward Elgar
Arr. by Rick Parks

9
Sw.
f
Ch.
12
15
17
Gt.

19
21
24
27
allargando
ff